Inner Monologues

L.D. Calica

BookLeaf
Publishing

India | USA | UK

Presentation by *BookLeaf Publishing*

Web: www.bookleafpub.com

E-mail: info@bookleafpub.com

ISBN: 9789363305922

First edition 2024

Prologue

An ancient bag of flesh and bones has awoken
from her slumber to the calling of Apollo,

Yes, I know, it is time.

A constant reminder that the cyclic thread of
time weaves in and out through us,
unbeknownst to us, we are at the mercy of Fate
herself.

Close your eyes and listen to Mother Earth.
Destiny is calling.

Experiences in this world, only one can dream
into existence.

My dearest grandchild, society paints us with a
colorblind theme. Remember the love that you
felt growing up with the family.

For when I am gone, I tell you this, you were
loved. Your innocence is budding. And how you
came to fruition was because I, too, was loved.

Many people will say, "I was loved once," but humanity has felt love.

Love comes in all shapes and sizes.
From the moment that we were conceived, we were loved.

The eternal bonds between a mother and father, mother and child, childhood friends, high school friendships, and sweethearts.

College lovers to online dating, humanity witnessed it all.

You alone, will be engulfed in an emotional rollercoaster, where these bonds will be made and broken all at once.

Leave no hatred or regret in your heart, for it will eat you alive.

And when you take your first step into the world, order a peach iced tea, my personal favorite, take a sip, and then you'll know why.

When the time is near, and you are old and gray
as I am, the dreams of the past will become your
comfort.

Life lessons. Even through death, love will find
a way to help you crawl out of the darkness.

A New Awakening

The rain washes away the fears and passions a
person may have.
It may also bring light to those who choose to
stand alone, stand above all the rest.

I am a Leo, I can stand on my own.

There have been changes and experiences and
differences of opinion in my life.
All of which I do not regret whatsoever, but
others may look down upon me and sigh.

Let me tell you then, that you no longer know
me, the person you knew before because I don't
know you either.

I am twenty-two years old, and I have a future to
look forward to, and there will be people that
stand in my way, and sadly I will be forced to
drop you.

I am stronger now, and I don't care what anyone

has to say to me. Yes, I'm not receptive to the world or voices that try to convince me otherwise.

This is my life, and I alone choose whether or not a person should be part of it.

These words reflect the idealist and realist that I am. It will be raw, it will be real, and enough of the bullshit games unless I post otherwise.

My business is my business, and people shouldn't stick their noses in where it doesn't belong, but am I contradicting myself by writing it down here?

Not necessarily. Of course, to know a person, you need only ask. That's all.

Why bother telling someone your life story when it goes in one ear and out the other?

I mean honestly, do you really give a shit about me? Doesn't it work both ways — a double-edged sword?

Grief and anger have prompted me to be more
focused and blunt with my words.
If I must put a fake smile on to counter the
nonsense around me, then I believe that will be
the case.

No one is perfect, that I can agree on, but to
continue the cycle of twisted tainted toxic
words, I think one should be executed by
default.

Only God can judge me, but I like playing the
role of Devil's advocate. To examine your life
outside the box, is more fulfilling than being
ignorant.

Can ignorance be bliss? Yes. But if you don't
know what you're talking about then you are
stupid.

So, let us all be carefree in our ways. Let us
move on toward truth and disgust for one other
because it's the only way.

Let us put love and indifference for one another
to the test. Let us bow out gracefully to the

world who failed to see who we really are,
but judged because of the sins we've committed.
Isn't this what human beings do? Time to smile
folks, let the games begin.

Untitled

Memories. Dreams. Reality.

To be completely stressed out from worry and failure can lead to one's downfall or in turn become yet another obstacle one has to face.

Looking at your options. What do you see? What does the world want you to see?

What are your goals and ambitions? For me, I would want to have things go my way. But I don't control fate, my decisions do.

A memory of dance. I close my eyes and my stress goes away. One of my favorite songs is playing and I can't help but feel secure and free once again.

The warmth and smile take me back to my little safety area, where my guard is down, and everything made sense at that very moment. One of my dreams will never be a reality. The power to lose oneself in art and expression.

Figures moving as one — a dance which I'd rather sway to and be lost in.

But reality snaps me back into things, and I wave goodbye to that image whenever I am down.

Restless Extension

Gaia wept upon the tainted ground with forceful,
toxic tears,
  Shouting toward her ungrateful human
children.
  "I AM DYING! DO YOU NOT HAVE ANY
COMMON SENSE?!"
  Oblivious, robotic, flesh-like, we were.

No answer ... until now ...

The laziness in our souls has been marinating
with despair, anxiety, and fear.
  But for those who have been in isolation from
the beginning,
  Laugh at the newcomers who've gone insane.

  Social distancing has been mastered by
introverts
  For those who seek solidarity.
  Be silent .. Be still.
  Libra tipped the scales — justice rewarded.

Let Nature run its course,
This was meant to be.
Life before humans ran
amok,
This was meant to be.

  As Gaia replenishes, her song calls out
To a multitude of entities.
  Before us, they were here.
  As we did not heed the calls.

Ignorance. Regret. Suffering.
Another restless extension.

Procrastination

Lost again in thoughts, this mind is running on
fumes
I'm no genie in a bottle, no wishes to grant
Years of torment locked away
In my heart, my mind. Just lost.

No physical pain can surpass the emotional jail
cell.
So let me be .. forever lost.
As I held out my hand to you — nothing,
Just a faint smile of my former self
Animated; drawn into the personalities
which juggle in countless directions. For all
time.

Nani? Nan desu ka? What? What is it?
God, I am so lost in this mess of
dreams—or were they nightmares?
Please wake me up from this utter boredom.
Should I pray later ... What should I do now?

Voiceless

Here I sit with so many thoughts in my mind
Always wondering where to go next.

Who am I today? Who am I to you?
They say that you don't know me until it's too
late
But then I never knew where I stood.

So many questions. So few answers.
Can you tell me .. was it worth it?

When I think about us, about the past, which
I'm trapped in. I figured it as much.

Too much time has passed and when I finally
opened up about you, the reality was that I did
love you.

I loved you for so long, for so many years and I
got played .. hard.
I dismissed the worthy ones around me. I waited

so long for you.
I told you how I felt
Yet my voice was never heard.
It was ignored by you.
You gave me the sad song of defeat.

The loophole of a dance in my heart and in my
head.
Those were my best memories of us.
And I still held on to them even after all this
time.
 Because I still don't know how to let it go. I've
longed for you while you disappeared.

Weaving in and out of my life without a care in
the world. Your dumb face and your half-ass
smile, I missed it.

 But you're gone now. We both moved on. Still
there are moments like this when I look up at the
sky and I dream that you're holding me and only
me.

No one else because I'm selfish like that. And
we danced to our song. That song that only I
knew so well.

There was a time

There was a time in this world where we would tell each other anything
No words or phrases that were too great
Only the words that the both of us needed to hear.

There was a time, when the love I have for you was enough
Enough to realize that shortly after, I wasn't enough.

There was a time, only moments ago when I heard from you
And you heard from me, where the reality sank in, my heart ached again.

There was a time, where insecurities arose, it could no longer be swept away But the painful reminder that the truth was waiting.

There was a time, where I held the dream of us so close

I could no longer breathe, and once more my
heart ached again.

  My extremities went numb, my mind kept
racing and turning
  Until I no longer saw who I was anymore, just
a fragment of a past life.

  There was a time, when I missed you and
longed for you
  But I was never enough.

  What can I possibly offer you, besides the
promise that I couldn't keep
  A promise that I continue to break as long as I
ever shall live.

  There was a time, when I closed my eyes, the
nightmares would dissipate
  And what was left, was the broken soul of a
lost woman.

  There was a time, when I no longer wanted to
survive
  Because the pain kept nagging and ripping
apart my flesh.

There was a time, when I longed for peace
In the midst of the chaos
To accept what will never come to pass.

There was a time, where auspices were a life
saver
Yet, not for this dreamer
Forgive me, for only now can I grant myself a
sigh of relief
As there was a time where I infinitely continue
to love you.

Orphans

The moment that I forget how far I've come
Is the minute I realize that you are no longer
here.

A solo heart breaks and yearns for wholeness
And here I am seeking answers from the
unknown.

It struck me today—again—where my tears
became a lost child.
And here I sit, hoping for this anguish to
subside into my subconsciousness.

How can a grown woman cry? It's easy, let me
tell you.
My aged worn glasses are splotchy from the
waterworks.
My fingers move intermittently as the mind
searches for answers, for words to say.

A product of orphans is who I am. Fable tales
were instilled in me. How you left home to

come to a new country, to start a new life for
yourself and your future family.

Both of you—selfish in a way aiming for your
dreams and desires.

And when that time came, a daughter was
born and taken at an age too young. She
departed from this mother earth to join the
angels in the great beyond,
And the title of Orphans became a scar in your
soul.

What was left? An eldest son and another baby
girl, born after the one that you lost. Time
flowed as it should.

You've grown older and wiser and so have the
children. No inkling or hint of what will come to
pass.

Only the hour of a twenty-one-year-old knew
life will no longer be the same.
The world that she knew as a child was no
longer hers. She had to grow up.

There was no choice. It was a matter of
survival.

Time spun again. Seven years from each other,
this daughter lost not only
A father but also a mother. Daddy's little girl;
tough love yet best friend mother-daughter
combo.

I became you. Orphans. My brother and myself.
Fending for survival. Reaching for the
impossible.

It still stings, you know, being an orphan.
Searching for an answer to "Why me?"

My whole family are orphans. The people that I
met and encounter are orphans to their own
demise.
I am a product of orphans. I am different. I am
unique.

Let me harness the pain that I felt during this
time
Spin it and create a new chapter.

Only Orphans have the instruction manual.
The manual to forge dreams and passions into
existence.

Is Enough, enough?

A stretched-out hand reaches out to the sky
It can be the roof over our heads or Earth's blue
bosom.
 This hand wavers through the images
 The sad tempo of a beating drum — a
heartbeat nonetheless.
 I close my eyes again and there you are.
Crying. Sobbing. The fear of loss. But it
happened.

 The non-dominant hand holding onto
an impossible task. Who will it be?

 In parallel realities, I've said "Yes" to each one,
the same one
 Over and over.

 Yet, here, I'm broken. You're broken.
Is enough, really enough?

 Things are supposed to happen after I'm
finished with my goal

But it never stops.

I'm still hungry. It's a hunger that I keep
yearning for.
Not maternalistic. More like an inner
satisfaction.
Angelica, you were right,
"I will never be satisfied."

Nine lives

I find myself deep in my thoughts about what
to write.
 Sometimes sitting down to take a piss
Or brushing my hair or moisturizing my
textured complexion of hybrid Asian.

 The Long Island girl who roams the city life in
all of its glory.
 It never takes much when I think of you. Of us.

 The dashing debonair smile, with the
child-like personality. Playful. Unimaginable. I
never grew up, did I? I'm still a child, the
outcast of society.

 A home, yes — several, actually. All waiting
for the presence of my mundane style
 Strict, forthcoming with beyond luxurious
appetite.

It seems unfair to sit here, imagining I have an
accent. Any freaking accent will do.

I guess the Long Island one is here to stay.

My crystals keep me company. So do my
plushies. They all have a purpose
  A symbol that only I can unlock.
  Will this lioness sleep well tonight? Or will my
thoughts swarm my synapses,
  Bend and break, flood them until daybreak? It's
too early though.
  Maybe midnight? Maybe I'll hear Johnny and
his fiendish escapades.

  Damn cats. They have nine lives. Why can't
humans have that option?
  A do-over. It's a crime, I say, to have that many
chances. It's a curse.
  Maybe that's why cats are the gatekeepers of
the underworld.
  Because they've seen some wild crap.

  Someday. It will be me. I will make it so.

Death's Door

A conversation between the Grim Reaper and a Soul:

Grim Reaper: Salutations! My dead friend. I see that you finally made it to the other side. Welcome!

Soul: Am I finally dead? Has my suffering ceased to exist?

GR: My friend, you are correct .. and I am here to collect you.

Soul: Collect me? You make it sound like you collect stamps or something.

GR: Meh .. more or less, if that's how you want to put it. It is a hobby after all. I am the one and only Grim Reaper! Although I must say, I get the bad rap for being portrayed a certain way, because of you know .. I look the way I look.

Soul: *(carefully looks at GR; nods in agreement)* Well, GR, you are not wrong about that. You do .. kind of look uninviting. I mean, you have no eyes .. and you carry a scythe that my ancestors would be fearful of.

GR: Well .. if I must explain, I can't always BE that ray of sunshine!! Listen, just like you, I was made this way.

Soul: So .. how does this work? Is there a rite of passage to go through the heavenly gates, or am I headed to the place that should not be named?

GR: HAHAHAHA! You mean, Hell?! Listen, my friend, I am here to guide you to your destination. Wherever you're supposed to go, you will go.
(GR and Soul were floating along the path)
First question, do you have any unfinished business?

Soul: Pardon?

GR: Do you feel like you deserved to die?
Ermm .. do you feel like you have accomplished
enough to pass on to your afterlife destination?

Soul: Well, I don't think I can say that. I mean,
I was ill with a terminal condition. I saw the
love of my life, my family, and spent the last
moments with them at home. My children, I
raised them the best that I could. I know that I
could have more time but I guess it was time. I
know that I had regrets, which I hope will not
haunt me for the rest of eternity. But to go back
.. in that sick body .. I'd rather be free from it. I
know now, what it means to suffer. And as
humans, we will go through it, but damn .. that
was a rough road. Long story short, GR, I gave
up hope and my body followed. That's mainly
the only regret that I have. But someday, I'll
meet my family again, and we'll be together
again. Right?

GR: My friend, I do want the best for you. The
Maitre D' will let you know at the gates.

Soul: Is this goodbye, GR?

GR: Hey .. I collect the souls and guide them to where they have to go. You can say, the "Bouncer of the Joint" will let you in.

Soul: Thanks, GR. You're not as bad as the world makes you out to be.

GR: I appreciate that. And remember .. have hope.

(As Soul waves goodbye to the Grim Reaper, they make their way toward the Gates of Light, carrying hope as they approach the Maitre D, to let them in)

(In return, the Grim Reaper delivers one of Earth's valuable possessions, dissipates in the distance, and continues its eternal duty of collecting souls)

Ramblings

No one tells you when you fall in love. No one ever explains to you how the process goes.

Puppy love. High school sweethearts. College sweethearts. Long distance love. Forbidden love.

Online dating. Dating in school. Friends with benefits that can either stay as that or become love.

Arranged marriages. Marriage dictated by family values. True love. The list goes on.

I know that I've missed more than I can remember. But this is it.

No one can tell you to stop loving the person that you are no longer with. No one can tell you that you shouldn't love more than one person.

As I have learned that loving more than one person is possible. It may not be the one you're meant to be with.. but you have companionship.

Friendship love. Friends first then lovers, then a partner in crime.

I am still learning to accept those conditions. I am still learning that I need to love myself more than others.

Because a broken heart is a broken soul, especially when it's you against the world.

I reflect on my shortcomings. What came to be and what once was. And that is how I live my life. It bothers me that it's never as "perfect" as how I want it to be.

I am angrier now because my patience runs thin. This is another thing that I have to change. Love myself more. Become less angry.

I need to learn to stress "less" over the little things because I know how important it is to pay attention to detail.

Did I confuse you my audience? Expect more of that. It's like when I take a shower or go for a walk and I have no way of writing it down.

Like this moment. I am laying in bed letting the thoughts run rampant and this is where they will stay.

Sun Time

Forgetful I had become. When darkness controls
my circadian rhythm to serve the sick and the
slumbering dreamers.

Routine is numbing. It is a task that has fallen
unto me, a task that has taken more than a
decade to fulfill.

Yet here I stand. Before you.
More like sitting under you. Not all eyes can
stare at you, we don't have the gifts to absorb
your enormous grace.
Far from it.

It has taken you a while to embrace me again.
To saturate this Morena with your
overwhelming light source.
Many names, we humans have given you.
But to me, you are the life-bringer, the center of
my solar sign—Apollo, Ra, Apolaki.

All nations have given you names .. but a
commoner calls you the Sun.

A Decennium Teaspoon

I defy all odds. I need to make it known.
It is a realization of being independent for such a
long time.

Before I was able to step into unwavering
experiences, my hand was forced and my
newfound chapter was postponed.

It was sheer blindness, a faint guiding light that
seemed too far to obtain.

Freedom from it all was what I can imagine.
"Just a little more," I said.. "It will be over
soon."

A decennium with a teaspoon. I lost them both
to Illness. Sadness. Depression.
The companions to this hostile heart. It was a
Catch-22.
I may become victorious at the end, but my
reflection overlooks the past.

Tunnel vision. This is what happens when
people are ghosted.

I literally tell them to "fuck off—you don't
understand what I've gone through."

It was the same sob story that I told.
And I got tired of making everyone happy.

There is no bitterness here. Acceptance, with a
touch of regret. But that is what life is.

It takes time to let go of regrets, but for me, it is
a matter of being released into the wild and
unknown.

To peek into the future with blind faith and take
hold of it and not let go.

Untitled

It finally hit me. I broke down but I didn't want
to say anything because saying it is repetitive.

Being "strong" doesn't get any easier.
Being in love and having hopes and dreams is
what keeps me going.
It sounds so cliché right now, but I don't care.

This is my life; this is what the big man up there
had planned for me or something similar to it.

From what people have told me, whether or not
it gets easier or if it's normal to feel this way,
I try to feel anything this Christmas, some sort
of normalcy.

Whether it's joy or sadness, just keeping my
mind busy on the next best thing and trying to
stay sane and not look like a lifeless soul.

I try to talk about my feelings but again, it's
redundant.
It's comforting to know that I have a place to go
to, even when my own house seems empty.

Transparency

It's been a minute since we crossed paths and
here we are again, but in a respectful manner.

 I was real and so were you. Missed a chance
but hey, things happen for a reason, right?

 For any dreamer of any industry, trying to put
out good family vibes to the community—is it
worth it?

 Can the classic, traditional, faith-driven soul be
convinced otherwise? We received our
blessings, one in many ways than we had
anticipated. A baby gain versus a baby loss.

 No human being can grant that deliverance yet
we see ourselves as playing God.

The tribal views do not haunt me; they're calling
out to me, telling me to wake up the fuck up.

In short, confessions were made, we kept it as real as we could.

At the end of the day, transparency, missed one shot, and yes, Eminem would be mad as hell.

Routine

The night before a work week, one can tell you they have become insane from a monotonous schedule.

Mondays. Poor Mondays. It never meant no harm. It's the universal day that starts the week either strong or as a shit show, and depending on the outcome, one may choose violence or peace.

Mondays can be a school day. Mondays for the working folk is another paycheck that goes out the window once bills start to complain.

Mondays are a routine—a routine that no one asked for.

Go to school. Get educated. Go to work. Become a zombie at work that you went to school for.

How to break the routine? Find the necessary nourishment around you. Find the purpose and fight till the end.

Subway Tuesdays

A typical stand on life where questionable individuals, dare not sit next to you, but scurry away like a dog, flicking its croc heels upward as if they were trying to mark their territory.

The female mammal protects its innocent face with a black mask, as if trying to make a statement.

Continuously playing musical chairs, shifting from a sitting to a standing position, speaking in a native tongue that is hard to distinguish.

Up and down, up and down, what spiritual being is she seeing? Is that strange?

As the rest of the world is glued to their handheld devices and silencers to block the natural waves of sound; the ability to listen to their environment is long gone.

Rise with the sun, prepare to be oppressed in our careers, go home in disbelief and failure.

What will this day bring today? If I knew that, I would have already told you by now, wouldn't I?

Carpe diem, grab your destiny by the horns and never let go. At least, not until you fall asleep.

I am today

It's my birthday today
And I'm crying.

Crying as I reflect on what I've accomplished
so far
And the losses that I had to endure.

When I think of Sad Sam and the one who gave
him to me,
He comes to mind and only him.

He will always be the first and last in my life,
in terms of endearment, and first love.

Days like this, especially with the rain today,
evoke a somber feeling rather than a celebration.

The tears and pain are real as every reflection
brings a memory of loss.

No physical parents to wish me a "Happy
Birthday". To remind me that I am getting older

or yell at me for no reason. Or to judge me
harshly for my decisions.

The past mistakes are long forgotten, moved
on to a world that we will remember but cannot
change.

The few that remain continue to hold a place,
somewhere in this empty void.

But remember, when you have nothing, there
is always something to look forward to.

I miss them. When memories of every little
detail flashes before your eyes including today,
it hurts, it really does.

The smiling faces and the pure joy of others
will continue to be a beacon of hope; they are
not physically here but it is a blessing.

Happy Birthday, to me, my memories, my past,
present, and future self.

Remember how you arrived here and remember
that you are lived, in life and in death.

A letter to those that remain

A blessing in disguise that the world stopped
for only a moment,
To let the disease pass and the obscurity linger

How troublesome would it have been if one's
parents remained to breathe?
The loneliness. The unknown. The torment of
the living, but thankfully they witnessed that
fate which many others had suffered. I am
grateful.

But for those that remain, how does it feel?
The youngest daughter among her siblings,
who spoke those solemn words, "Her? I don't
know her, that stupid girl."

But you do know who I am, now don't you,
Miss A. Imagine the shock on my face but with
that Anya smile, I know the truth about all of
you.

Miss A likes to put on a show for her mother,
blind but not deaf as she sat quietly and politely.
The foolish child must have forgotten her past.
Let these words remind you.

Money doesn't grow on trees, please stop
pretending. This applies to the rest of you.

Washington may be hidden under one's nose,
but with the sleight of hand, those slippery wet
fingertips will snatch treasure right where the
blind sit.
No foolish girl, we know that it was stolen. It
was Miss A all along.

The black sheep was the gentlest of creatures
but was scorned by her siblings because of bad
blood.
To her demise, the offspring suffered the same
fate.

Sniff-sniff. Smell that? It smells like raw
sewage to me.
Don't pretend that yours does not smell like that.

How does it feel to be a side dish to the main
course? Imagine waiting for a cold dead fish to
be thrown out, all because the guest preferred
the main course to be a well-done filet mignon.

Gross.

The offspring are kept in the dark, sad but true.
Every generation should know this:
all the men and women indirectly made a name
for themselves at the Red-Light
  District.

  Oh, the lies that people told us, including the
  Marites, when one proclaimed that my mother
was a second mother to all of you.
To this day, I find that hard to believe.

  Moses gave me a glimpse of what he saw, he
spoke to God and received the Ten
Commandments. Seven deadly sins. Lies.
Coveted husbands and wives. Stolen goods,
more lies.

  Here lies the gamblers, who showed no effort in
how they arrived here, only a silver spoon in

their mouths and asses. Good for you, I say! But shame on everyone!

The audacity of forgetfulness that these fools have taken for granted. Remember how you crossed those torrential seas, the arrival of the bitter cold nipping at your doorstep?

The endless lines and parchment stamped to bring every living soul here, so you may be able to see the light at the end of the tunnel.

Truth be told, she should have left you to starve and become poor. Only then, when the Marites become humble. Now look at these gluttonous simpletons, obese, old and decrepit.

The one with the broken heart, how is that going for you? I have yet to receive a legitimate answer from you.

I guess my tears did not touch your cold-hearted soul. Another disappointment.

The one who is afraid of everything. Endless
calls from both the living and the dead.
It must be nice to ignore a dead niece. Do I
remind you of her? Since we are pretending,
continue to believe that your betrothed loves
you, she does not and never will.

The third in command, the gambler. Still the
same I see. I can't wait to listen to your useless
ignorance and deceitfulness.

The second-in-line, the jester, the mind-control,
the witch who bore her offspring, demon's
blood, tainted in the bloodline. This soul can
feel and smell the Grinch's smile on your face
along with Marcos. Two peas in a pod, the one
who used to be like the Flintstones.

It only took one mango to create a domino
effect, along with the truth and lies. How does
it feel to declare Martial Law within your
family?

The angel wanted peace but the villain needed
her hands dirty. What a shame.

War was declared.

A never-ending battle, bloodied war. He who
wears the crown has deemed themselves to be
king and ruler of these lands but I call upon all
those that are holy, our pagan gods before Christ
the Savior, the ghosts of the past and your
beloved God, Gabriel and Lucifer.

The flames of Pompeii demolished a city as
it engulfed its history, its everlasting glory.
Our paths will cross, I am hopeful that your
demise would be just.

And don't forget that being second may hold
value, but sadly, number one was taken too
soon. You will never be her.

The baby asked to be loved by his siblings but
was heavily ignored by them. His wife pleaded
but he refused.

Death was waiting for him. Initially, he was
loved but not since that day. His eldest spoke the
words, "Where were you when we were here?

He needed you more than he did us. He was left alone, once again."

Two and eleven. Three and number two's spouse, how ironically compatible. To share the same lying despicable bloodline.

The one that talked too much had the most truth out of everybody. Respect is in order.

Open Arms

Fear is that I will wake up from a terrible
nightmare,
In a panic state, delirious and lost.

Independent to dependent,
I've almost lost my composure and sensibility.

Questions from the past rekindle a sparked
curiosity,
Who am I to you?

And what was the answer that I've long sought
after?

There is no comparison needed, for I have
found what I was searching for.
There is no desire to seek another.

Ambitious and daring for the constant need for
attention,
Which was beyond satisfactory.

How many times have I pushed you away and
yet you remained—
Here, close enough, but distant because I lack
the confidence in myself.

I had become a wandering gypsy, always
moving toward an unreachable star. And
yet, here you are, intact and unhinged,
waiting with open arms.

It was then that I knew,
I had found joy, in an unlikely turn of events,
A partner that embraced total chaos and calmed
it with unconditional love.

I felt safe. I can breathe again.
I will remind Fate to steer clear of my destiny,
For I am an unstoppable force.

I will turn my dreams into reality, And
you will be there by my side for all of
eternity.

I love you.

9 789363 305922